UNDERSTANDING SUICIDE

UPFRONT HEALTH

Published in the United States of America by Cherry Lake Publishing
Ann Arbor, Michigan
www.cherrylakepublishing.com

Reading Adviser: Marla Conn MS, Ed., Literacy specialist, Read-Ability, Inc.

Photo Credits: ©aldomurillo/Getty Images, cover; ©MrPants/Getty Images, 1;
©PeopleImages/Getty Images, 5; ©sharply_undone/Getty Images, 9; ©Mike Windle/Getty
Images, 10; ©skaman306/Getty Images, 12; ©Antonio_Diaz/Getty Images, 15; ©graphixchon/
Getty Images, 19; ©Steve Debenport/Getty Images, 20; ©yacobchuk/Getty Images, 21;
©omgimages/Getty Images, 23; ©GeorgiaCourt/Getty Images, 25; ©arsenik/Getty Images,
27; ©martin-dm/Getty Images, 28; ©Mike Windle/Getty Images, 30

Library of Congress Cataloging-in-Publication Data has been filed and is available
at catalog.loc.gov

Cherry Lake Publishing would like to acknowledge the work of the Partnership for 21st
Century Learning.
Please visit *www.p21.org* for more information.

Printed in the United States of America
Corporate Graphics

ABOUT THE AUTHOR

Matt Chandler is the author of more than 35 nonfiction children's books. He lives in
New York with his wife Amber and his children Zoey and Oliver. When he isn't busy
researching or writing his next book, Matt travels the country bringing his school author
visits and writing workshops to elementary and middle school students.

TABLE OF CONTENTS

CHAPTER 1

Examining Suicide

Kate Spade was wealthy and famous. Her designer handbags were carried by women all over the world. She seemed to have it all. But in 2018, the celebrity designer hung herself in her New York City apartment. Her husband says Spade had suffered from anxiety and depression for years.

One of the biggest contributing factors to a person's decision to take their own life is mental illness. People suffering from depression, anxiety, or schizophrenia may feel they have no other options. In the case of Kate Spade, she may have felt it was too difficult to keep living.

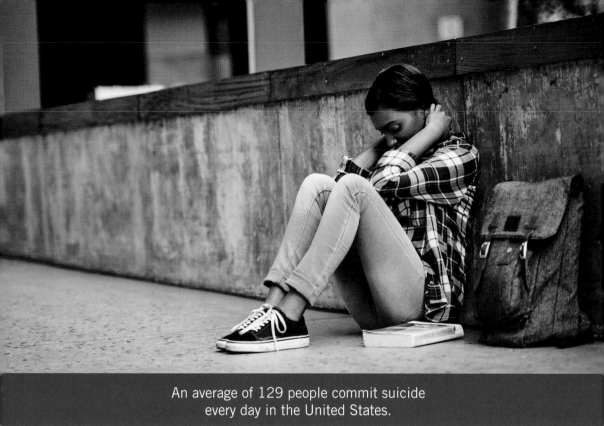

An average of 129 people commit suicide
every day in the United States.

There are many options to treat mental illness. Medications, therapy, and even hospitalization may be needed. Unfortunately, many people never get the help they need. It is estimated that 50 percent of the people suffering from mental illness are either undiagnosed or untreated.

Nearly 800,000 people commit suicide each year across the globe. That is 1 person every 40 seconds. Experts estimate there may be 20 times as many suicide attempts. For young people ages 15 to 29, suicide is the second leading cause of death.

Reaching Out

People who choose to commit suicide feel like there are no options left. They isolate themselves from the people who care about them. But preventing suicide may be as simple as talking with someone. Sometimes that could be a parent or close family member. You might have a favorite teacher or a school counselor you can confide in. Those around you can't help if they don't know how you feel. Talking is an important first step in getting help to deal with suicidal thoughts.

Suicide has also been used throughout history by people suffering from medical conditions. A patient who has cancer or is paralyzed may see death as a better option than living in sickness. This has led to a political debate over **physician-assisted suicide**. Today seven states and Washington, DC, allow a **terminally ill** patient to end their life by suicide. This usually involves a doctor prescribing a lethal dose of medication to end the patient's life.

As people get older, financial stress and job loss are often seen as possible triggers for suicide. There have even been cases of teens being bullied who committed suicide.

Suicide in the United States is on the rise. The number of people killing themselves has risen by 30 percent in the last 20 years. Men commit suicide far more often than women. Suicide is a permanent response to what is often a temporary problem.

Suicide Globally

Suicide impacts people across the globe. According to the **World Health Organization**, nearly 80 percent of all suicides occur in countries of lower or middle-class income earners. People with less money often have less access to good health care, including mental health counseling. This may contribute to their increased risk for suicide. In 2015, a study examined the countries with the highest rates of teen suicide (ages 15 to 19). The top countries were New Zealand, Iceland, Latvia, Estonia, and Canada. Do some research. What do these countries have in common that might contribute to their suicide rates? Greece had the lowest suicide rate. What do you think makes Greece different?

CHAPTER 2

A Permanent Response to a Temporary Problem

Life is full of second chances. Fail a test, and there will be another to improve on. Get cut from a team, and you can try out again next season. But there are no second chances with suicide. There is no coming back or changing your mind. Ask an adult you know if their life today is different than it was 10 years ago or 20 years ago. The answer will be "yes." Life is constantly changing. The struggles you have today will be replaced with opportunities tomorrow. The bully will go away. The friend that hurts you and walks away will be replaced by a new friend. When someone is in a lot of physical or emotional pain, it can be hard to see that bright future. It can be hard to imagine a time when the hurt is gone.

Making mistakes and overcoming challenges builds character, making people stronger and more resilient in the long run.

Patrick McCalley was a 17-year-old high school junior in the fall of 2016. He had a family who loved him. He had a girlfriend. He earned great grades in school. Patrick was planning to possibly join the U.S. Air Force when he graduated. Unfortunately, he got into trouble at school and faced a suspension. McCalley responded by leaving school and committing suicide.

Steven Spielberg was bullied as a kid, and his parents divorced when he was a teenager.

Experts say one of the challenges with teens is that their brains aren't fully developed. This can lead to **impulsive** decision-making. In Patrick McCalley's case, the discipline would have been a minor setback to his future. But in the moment, he could not see past the immediate pain and worry to visualize the bright future that was ahead.

Fifteen-time Grammy Award winner Adele was once suspended from her high school for fighting. She went on to sell more than 100 million albums. Steven Spielberg was rejected multiple times when he applied for college at the University of Southern California. He went on to direct films that have earned more than $10 billion at the box office! Everyone makes mistakes. Everyone has struggles. When times are tough, it is important to look for the good things in life and expect a better future.

Missing Out

In 2012, a Canadian teenager named Amanda Todd took her own life after suffering through years of bullying. What if Amanda had been able to look past high school? She might have seen a life where the bullies were gone. A life where she had a great job and lots of friends that loved her. A life where the bullying was a distant memory. What other things do you think a person misses out on when they commit suicide? What are some of the things you are looking forward to experiencing as you get older?

Prescription pills, many of which can be lethal, can be found in most homes in the United Stares.

Methods Matter

In the United States, there are three primary methods people use to commit suicide. Roughly 16 percent of people use pills or poison. Approximately 25 percent of people hang themselves or suffocate. But firearms are the most common method of suicide. More than half of all suicides in the United States involve the use of a gun. One reason for this is availability. It is estimated that Americans own more than 300 million guns. Millions of those guns are left unlocked where teens can access them. In 2016, 633 children ages 10 to 17 died by gun-related suicide.

This chart shows the rate of suicide among young people, broken down by age group and gender for 2016, the most recent year complete data was available.

Source: Data/chart from the World Health Organization website.

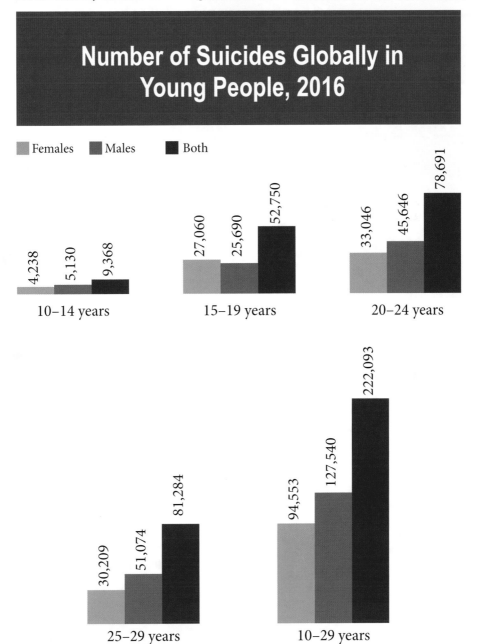

Number of Suicides Globally in Young People, 2016

■ Females ■ Males ■ Both

10–14 years
4,238 5,130 9,368

15–19 years
27,060 25,690 52,750

20–24 years
33,046 45,646 78,691

25–29 years
30,209 51,074 81,284

10–29 years
94,553 127,540 222,093

Teen Suicide

Suicide among teenagers rose 70 percent between 2006 and 2016. White males between the ages of 14 and 21 are the most at-risk. Suicide among black teens rose 77 percent during the same period. Teen suicide is preventable. Prevention begins with figuring out why so many young people are seeing suicide as their only option.

The unfortunate truth is, no one knows exactly what is causing the rise in teen suicides, but there are some ideas. One researcher at San Diego State University believes there is a link between smartphone use and the anxiety and depression that can lead to suicide. **Psychologist** Jean Twenge found that teens who spend 5 or more hours on their phone per day are 71 percent more likely to have a risk factor for suicide.

Teens who spend a lot of time on social media sites may have up to 66 percent higher rates of depression.

The pressure to "fit in" has always been part of being a teenager. But in the world of social media and smartphones, teens are constantly comparing their lives to those they see constructed on social media. This can increase feelings of depression, anxiety, and worthlessness. And even with its many benefits, a smartphone is no substitute for in-person interactions with friends and family.

Careers in Mental Health

There is help out there for people who are struggling. There are many careers for people who specialize in suicide prevention. Mental health experts believe as many as 70 percent of suicide victims suffered from a mental or emotional **disorder***. Psychologists,* **psychiatrists***, and licensed mental health counselors are all trained to help people with mental or emotional challenges. School guidance counselors are also trained to talk with teens who are struggling with thoughts of suicide. Would you ever like to have a job like this? Do you think it would be rewarding to help people feel better?*

Another possible factor for the increase in teen suicide is brain development. The human brain grows and develops at different speeds. Two areas of the brain are responsible for your feelings and emotions, including acting impulsively. They are called the hippocampus and amygdala. They mature very quickly. Unfortunately, the part of the brain that regulates impulses and balances things out does not. The prefrontal cortex doesn't fully develop until a person is about 25 years old. This could be a risk factor for teens. A teen who experiences sudden trauma may act on his emotions because his prefrontal cortex isn't developed enough to keep those impulsive decisions, like suicide, in check.

Whatever the cause behind the rise in suicide, doctors, scientists, and researchers are working to find solutions.

Teens Helping Teens

Talking to the adults in your life can be helpful sometimes. Other times, it feels good to talk to people your own age. Teen support groups are growing in popularity.

Many cities also offer in-person teen-led support groups. Teens are free to share their stories and get advice from other teens. This also gives teens a chance to connect with other young people who may have gone through similar experiences.

Teen Line (teenlineonline.org) is a California-based organization dedicated to connecting teens with teens. They have trained teenagers ready to help. You can call, e-mail, or text them, and they will listen!

CHAPTER 4

Solving Suicide

If there is no single reason causing so many people to take their own lives, how can we fix this **epidemic**? Lowering the number of suicides begins with early **intervention**. Eight out of 10 people who commit suicide show some warning signs before they act on it. Parents, teachers, friends, and coworkers need to watch for signs. Don't be afraid to ask questions if something doesn't seem right. If a person seems suicidal, you can even ask them directly if they are feeling like harming themselves. Maybe you notice a friend or coworker who seems depressed. They might be missing school or work and seem withdrawn. Talk to them. Ask how they are feeling. Encourage them to share their feelings. Talking to a person about suicide does not increase the chances they will harm themselves. Just

About 60 percent of people who have committed suicide were experiencing major depression at the time.

the opposite. Many people who are suicidal feel isolated and alone. Being there for a person in crisis can make a difference.

The worst thing you can do is ignore a person who is talking about harming themselves. Some people believe talking about suicide is a way for a person to get attention. They assume the person will never actually do it. The truth is, most people show warning signs of suicide before they ever attempt it. Those warnings can include directly talking about ending their life. Treat even the smallest remark about self-harm as a cry for help. The person has confided in you because they need your help.

Therapists can help people manage suicidal thoughts by providing coping strategies and ways to distract themselves.

That help sometimes means you need to talk to an adult. Your friend may have sworn you to secrecy. They may have made you promise you wouldn't tell anyone. But a person who is threatening suicide needs help. Sometimes they need more help than a friend can give. You might feel like you are breaking their trust or you are a bad friend if you tell an adult. You're not. You care about your friend, and you are making sure they get the help they need. Whether it is a teacher, school counselor, or parent, tell a trusted adult what you know and ask them to help. You might save a life.

[21ST CENTURY SKILLS LIBRARY]

Advanced technology such as brain monitoring might become a tool for doctors to monitor and diagnose suicide risk.

The Science of Your Brain

Can doctors study your brain and predict if you might commit suicide? A group of American researchers believe they can. The researchers studied the brains of people who had attempted suicide and compared them to people who had never considered suicide. The subjects were shown a series of words, and their brain's reactions to the words were monitored. Those reactions were then analyzed using an **algorithm** designed to predict the likelihood that the person had suicidal tendencies. The computer program correctly identified 94 percent of the suicidal participants!

Cyberbullying and Suicide

Social media is an important part of many people's lives, but it can also be dangerous. Social media sites can be great ways to show friends what you are doing. They can also be used to harass and hurt people. People who may never bully someone in person might send a hurtful text or social media message. They might start a group chat to spread lies about a classmate. **Cyberbullying** is a serious concern. One study in England found that young people who are cyberbullied are twice as likely to attempt suicide.

Researchers studied 41 suicides of children between ages 13 and 18 where cyberbullying was involved. In 78 percent of those cases, the victims were also bullied in school.

If you were cyberbullied, who would you go to for help? Having a plan to deal with social media bullies can make you better prepared to handle cyberbullying if it happens to you.

About half of teens experience cyberbullying at some point.

Getting Help

It is very rare for a single issue to cause someone to take their own life. Let's look at some of the most common contributing factors to suicide and see how a person can get help before it's too late.

Depression/anxiety: Depression is more than just feeling sad. It is a mental disorder than can impact every aspect of a person's life. For some people, meeting with a trained therapist and talking about their life can help. A counselor can offer strategies to manage depression. For others, taking medication prescribed by a doctor can help regulate depression or anxiety.

Bullying/cyberbullying: Bullying has been linked to many high-profile suicides in recent years. If you are being bullied, you need to protect yourself. Do what you can to avoid the

Teens who are gay, shy, socially awkward, or have learning disorders are bullied more often than others.

bully. If you are being bullied in school, immediately tell a teacher. If you are being cyberbullied, block the person on your social media account and tell your parents.

Relationship problems: Breaking up with a boyfriend or girlfriend can be heartbreaking. A person who experienced a bad breakup is **vulnerable**. The person should stay active and social. Making plans with friends is one idea. Being around other people can help. It can also help to remind the person that the sadness they are feeling is just temporary.

Hotlines for Help

When a person is in crisis, it can feel like no one around them understands. Thankfully, there are other options. Suicide hotlines have been around since the 1960s. Trained operators will listen to a person share their story. They can also offer directions for finding available services in your area. For some people, having a caring person on the phone to listen can be a great comfort.

In the United States:
National Suicide Prevention Hotline: 800-273-8255
Crisis Text Line: Text 741741

In Canada:
Crisis Services Canada: 833-456-4566
Crisis Text Line: Text 45645

Financial problems: The loss of a job or deep credit card debt can fuel depression and anxiety. If a person believes they can no longer provide for themselves or their family, suicide may feel like the only option. It isn't. Financial counselors are available for free in many cases. They can offer people options to fix the financial mess they are in.

Middle-aged white men have the highest suicide rates in the United States. Experts think this is due to the stress of the troubled economy.

With the help of friends, family, and professionals, most people recover from having suicidal thoughts.

Help is always available, and every life is valuable and worth living. If you know someone who is suffering, reach out and be there for them. If you are suffering and considering harming yourself, tell someone you care about. Call a hotline. Talk to a teacher. Suicide isn't a solution to a problem. It is a tragic decision no one needs to make.

Warning Signs

There are some signs you can look for that may let you know someone is considering suicide.

Sadness: Long periods of sadness or depression that doesn't seem to improve can be a warning sign.

Withdrawal from family and friends: A person who is usually social and friendly may suddenly lose interest in being with friends and family.

Dangerous behavior: Someone who is planning to take their own life may act dangerously. They won't care about their safety if they are planning to die.

Changes in appearance: A person in despair may not shower or groom themselves. They may wear the same clothes and appear to give up on how they look.

Preparing for the end: Sometimes a person planning to die will make preparations. They might visit their close friends and appear to be saying goodbye. They might give away treasured possessions and avoid making plans for the future.

As a kid, Steven Spielberg was bullied for being awkward, Jewish, and bad at sports. He was later diagnosed with dyslexia. Dyslexia is a condition that makes it hard to read and write. As a young adult, Spielberg started making movies. It was a great way to use his skills. He felt good about himself and was able to overcome the bullying.

Using the internet or the library, research other famous people who have overcome challenges like Spielberg. Did they overcome bullying or mental health issues? How were they able to get past difficult times? Can you use their approach in your own life?

Learn More

BOOKS

Cartlidge, Cherese. *Teens and Suicide*. San Diego: ReferencePoint Press, 2017.

Marsico, Katie. *The World Health Organization*. Ann Arbor, MI: Cherry Lake Publishing, 2015.

Pack-Jordan, Erin. *Everything You Need to Know About Suicide and Self-Harm*. New York: Rosen Young Adult, 2019.

Roland, James. *Careers in Mental Health*. San Diego: ReferencePoint Press, 2017.

ON THE WEB

Suicide Prevention Resource Center—Resources for Teens
https://www.sprc.org/resources-programs/suicide-prevention-resources-teens

TeensHealth—Suicide
https://kidshealth.org/en/teens/suicide.html

Teen Mental Health
http://teenmentalhealth.org

GLOSSARY

algorithm (AHL-go-rih-them) a set of rules for solving a problem in a set number of steps, often used by computer programs

cyberbullying (SY-buhr-bul-lee-ing) the act of posting insulting, embarrassing, or hurtful messages or photos of another person on the internet

disorder (dis-OR-dur) a mental or physical illness

epidemic (ep-i-DEM-ik) a health crisis that affects many people at once

impulsive (ihm-PUHL-sihv) taking action involuntarily or without thinking it through

intervention (in-ter-VEN-shen) getting involved in a situation, usually to offer assistance

physician-assisted suicide (FIZ-ish-uhn-uh-SIS-tid SOO-uh-side) when a doctor provides a patient with the information and ability to end their own life, usually by providing medication and information on a lethal dose

psychiatrist (sye-KYE-uh-trist) a doctor who treats people with mental and emotional issues, usually by prescribing medication

psychologist (sye-KOH-luh-jihst) a doctor who treats people with mental and behavioral issues, usually by trying to change their behavior

terminally ill (TUHR-mih-nuhl-lee IL) having an illness that cannot be cured and will cause death

vulnerable (VUHL-nur-uh-buhl) open to attack or being hurt emotionally, mentally, or physically; unable to easily defend oneself

World Health Organization (WURLD HELTH or-guh-nuh-ZAY-shuhn) a United Nations agency in charge of overseeing international public health

INDEX